Replaced *with* Grace

Leanne Harrington

WESTBOW°
PRESS
A DIVISION OF THOMAS NELSON
& ZONDERVAN

Revised Standard Version of the Bible, copyright 1952 [2nd edition, 1971] by
the Division of Christian Education of the National Council of the Churches of
Christ in the United States of America. Used by permission. All rights reserved.

WestBow Press books may be ordered through booksellers or by contacting:

WestBow Press
A Division of Thomas Nelson & Zondervan
1663 Liberty Drive
Bloomington, IN 47403
www.westbowpress.com
1 (866) 928-1240

Because of the dynamic nature of the Internet, any web addresses or
links contained in this book may have changed since publication and
may no longer be valid. The views expressed in this work are solely those
of the author and do not necessarily reflect the views of the publisher,
and the publisher hereby disclaims any responsibility for them.

Any people depicted in stock imagery provided by Thinkstock are
models, and such images are being used for illustrative purposes only.
Certain stock imagery © Thinkstock.

ISBN: 978-1-4908-5087-0 (sc)

Library of Congress Control Number: 2014915945

Printed in the United States of America.

WestBow Press rev. date: 9/23/2014

Dedication

*W*ith God as my guide He asked me to write this book. After I came into His church, He taught me to rely on His Word. I learned to find answers to questions by looking in the Bible. Since His request, I've filled blank pages with my testimony, portraying my circumstances, my dysfunctional life, and my poor choices. You'll read about my insane lifestyle; doing the same thing over and over expecting different results.

But, He didn't ask me to write this to tell you about me; He wants me to tell you about Him. Step 12 says, having had a spiritual awakening as a result of these steps, we tried to carry this message to alcoholics and to practice these principles in all our affairs. In Luke 15:3-10 the Revised Standard Version states, so he told them this parable: "What man of you, having a hundred sheep, if he has lost one of them, does not leave the ninety-nine in the wilderness, and go after the one which is lost, until he finds it? And when he has found it, he lays it on his shoulders, rejoicing. And when he comes home, he calls together his friends and his neighbors, saying to them, 'Rejoice with me, for I have found my sheep which was lost.'

Just so, I tell you, there will be more joy in heaven over one sinner who repents than over ninety-nine righteous persons who need no repentance.

He healed me. I've been recreated. He gave me His free gift of grace; He granted me my childhood dream. This book is my gift to Him. I'm sharing Him with you. If at first you don't have a relationship with God or have some uncertainty around building a relationship with Him; just wait. He was guiding me way before I knew it. If you open your heart just a little, before you know it, He will be your guide too.

"*H*i. My name is Leanne and I'm an Adult Child of an Alcoholic." She said.

"Hi Leanne," The whole room replied.

Could everyone in the room hear her heart pounding against her rib cage? She looked around the room as the facilitator got seated. These meetings were always in the basement. The materials and the coffee were set up on a table in the back of the room with the posters hung behind the speaker. Some rooms are too bright and some too dim, some rooms are too big and some not big enough. The old wooden chairs creaked and scraped across the hardwood floor. The smell of freshly brewed coffee distracted her to a vision of her backyard from the rocker on her deck. Smiling, she relaxed as a peaceful feeling swept over her. She glanced at the one item hanging on the community bulletin board and then looked into the faces in the front row. The room was silent.

"Thank you so much for asking me to share my story tonight. It's my pleasure to be with all of you; I am so glad you are here. Would you all please take a moment of silence and we will follow it with the serenity prayer."

How long is a moment of silence? At some meetings, the moment lasts five to ten seconds. It's so quick; a person barely has time to say, "Dear Heavenly Father…" Depending on the speaker, a moment might drag on awkwardly for what seems like hours. She used the time for prayer; a time to contact her higher power and ask Him to speak through her. After a couple of minutes, she finished her prayer and broke the silence with the word God and the group delivered the serenity prayer like a well orchestrated chorus singing Christmas carols.

"I want to thank my higher power, whom I choose to call God, for the privilege of standing in front of you tonight. My recovery date is June 2, 2009. It is by the grace of God that I was led to these halls and I give Him all the glory for leading me into His church. I'm speaking to you tonight based on the second tradition of Alcoholics Anonymous and Al-anon. Will you say Tradition Two with me? 'For our group purpose there is but one ultimate authority—a loving God as He may express Himself in our group conscience. Our leaders are but trusted servants; they do not govern.'

I am here only as a messenger of our God Almighty; may my story plant a seed in you that will blossom into a flower of hope. I am grateful for His guided journey and for the gifts He's given to me. As a child, I hated my life. My biggest dream, my passion, was to experience grace. I used the word normal back then; any improvement in my life would classify it as normal. I spent a lifetime searching, ignoring God's attempts to contact me. Ignore may be the wrong word; I didn't recognize He was trying to contact me. However, in 2 Peter 3:9 Revised Standard Version (RSV) it states the Lord is not slow about his promise as some count slowness, but is forbearing toward you, not wishing that any should perish, but that all should reach repentance. The Lord was as patient with me as He was with the people being led out of the land of Egypt.

they were new to recovery. The first step can be as simple as showing up. She remembered reaching stalemate in her own damaged relationships. Her thought shattered when someone in the opposite corner sneezed and rustled in their chair.

"My instructions say I'm to share with you what my life was like, what brought me to recovery and explain what my life is like today. We all have our own journeys and I'm going to start you with a glimpse of my childhood years. Unfortunately, both of my parents have passed away. God helped me forgive and release the blame I placed on them for so many years. I will do my best to stay focused on how I was affected emotionally and spiritually growing up in their household. God helps us see the truth about ourselves, leaving others in His hands. I looked up statistics gathered by the Alabama Coalition Against Domestic Violence. It reports that children exposed to domestic violence show internalized and externalized behavior problems which can become extreme and dangerous when they reach adolescents. Young people may use drugs or alcohol and be involved in truancy or gangs. They may act out sexually which may involve pregnancy. Some runaway or become suicidal.

I was three or four year's old, playing outside, when my father drove in the yard. As the car door shut, I hollered, "Hi Daddy." He marched to the front door, onto the porch and into the house without speaking to me. I heard him shouting at my mother. I heard my mother crying. I had to go pee and tried to open the door but it was locked. I banged on the door, but no one came. The lawn was mowed in front of the house, but not off to the side. I walked into the jungle of tall grass, pulled down my pants and peed. I was embarrassed. I was standing in the walkway when he slammed the porch door, got into his car and backed out of the driveway. I ran into the house. My mother stood next to the kitchen table with tears streaming down her face. The pearl white strip of buttons was ripped off the front of her blouse and hanging down to her knees. My embarrassment switched to an overwhelming desire to comfort her. Crying, she asked, "What did I do? What did I do?" Without realizing it, I became my mother's caretaker. Each and every time my father beat her up, I would go to her and she would ask me for advice regarding what she did wrong. I literally tried to answer that question for her. This became love for me; my mother needed me.

While my father was building our new house, I started school, my younger brother was born, my grandfather bought me a brand new bike and I got bit by a wild mouse. We watched our cat get run over, a bat got stuck on the porch, my babysitter got killed in a car crash and my tongue got stuck to an electric meter box while I licked the fresh new snow off the top. I fell down and hit my head on the ice twice that same winter and that was the one time I remember my father hugging me. At my great grandmother's house, I teamed up with a friend to beat the cabbages in the neighbor's garden. We were made to apologize to the neighbor. While visiting my parents' friends, a horse reared and his front feet were just above my head. A pair of arms grabbed me and whisked me out of the way before the horse landed on me. Later in life I learned it was a pony.

One year at Christmas we were living with my great grandmother. My parents were separated. My father came by to visit. He was on crutches. I remember asking, "Daddy, what happen?" He said, "I went for a ride with Santa in his sleigh and I fell out." I was three or four years old and I believed him. I was concerned for him. Years later my mother told me he got into a fight with another guy.

God tried to contact me through my great grandmother. I would spend hours upside down on her couch looking at the crystal icicles hanging from the lamp above my head singing "Mine Eyes Have Seen the Glory". She loved to hear me sing. I sang in the choir at the church across the street and went to Sunday school until I was nine years old. Revelation 3:20 says, 'Behold, I stand at the door and knock; if any one hears my voice and opens the door, I will come in to him and eat with him, and he with me.' I didn't hear his knock.

When I was eight years old we moved into our new house and I got my very own room. Over the next few years we experienced increased chaos. Almost every holiday my father would get drunk and by the time we ate he would pass out; sometimes with his head in his plate. We continued eating like nothing was wrong. On some of the summer holiday cookouts he would get into shouting matches with my aunts or uncles and they would leave mad. I remember watching at one gathering; he stood inside the open car door of my aunt's car, on the driver's side in his bare feet on the tar driveway. He braced himself with one arm on the door and the other up over the driver's head trying to stop her from backing up. She revved the motor, inching the car back, while they were both hollering at each other. He finally stepped away from the car and she left. He was left standing alone wobbling drunk in the driveway.

Even though I was embarrassed, fearful and felt hatred toward my father, I also admired him. He built our house, he fixed our cars, he landscaped, he fished, he hunted, he taught us about nature, he was creative and he could draw. He always photographed us and created home movies with an early version of the camcorder. We watched these movies on a screen and a reel-to-reel projector. They were silent movies. One year for Christmas I got a camera. Without my mother telling me she made my father do the shopping, I knew it came from him. I started photographing my life.

One summer we camped at a seasonal lot in a nearby town. They worked different shifts and drove back and forth to work from there so we kids got to live there for the whole summer. One evening my mother was working and we were hanging with Dad. He always planted a garden and had brought one of those big brown grocery bags full of peas that needed to be hulled. My father asked my older brother and I to take the peas out of their pods while he and our younger brother went visiting. My brother and I got quite a bit done, but were jealous they were playing and we were not. We strewed the rest of the bag of peas into the woods and down squirrel holes and left to join them. He questioned us and we lied. Later that evening when we got back to the camp lot, he was on to us and found the pea pods in the woods. He put us over his knee by the campfire and beat our bare butts with a one inch square dowel. I had strips of purple bruises across my legs and bottom for quite some time. I hurt; I couldn't sit down.

I was ashamed and embarrassed. My inner alarm was fully charged every day. I paid attention to routine trying to predict the calm as well as the storm. My chores were always inspected and I was made to re-do the whole chore if one dish had soap on it or if I missed sweeping under a chair. I clung to my mother when she was home; traveling with her whenever she did errands. I molded my behavior trying to be perfect; trying to please.

Has anyone seen the Facebook posts about a Buddy Bench? A second grader came up the idea so students never felt left out on the playground. If you sit on the bench, another student will go to the bench to see if you want to talk or play. I sure wish we had these when I was in elementary school. I remember walking around the playground all bundled up in my winter clothing. I was all alone. I felt alone. I felt no one liked me. I felt unwanted. I wanted attention. I wanted someone to love me.

I spent many nights hiding under my covers listening to loud voices and screams with an occasional whack of a solid object against another solid object. I would jump. I couldn't sleep. In the quiet of the next morning a broomstick without the broom lay on the kitchen table. We would find gobs of hair on the floor. Dad would enter the kitchen while I was getting a bowl of cereal. He'd say good morning like nothing happen. I'd say hi back like nothing happen.

My dreams started taking shape at this point. I declared I was going to go to college. No one in the family had gone to college. My parents fought about money and I was never going to be in my mother's situation. She was always asking for money, being told she spent too much of it and told she couldn't have any more. I remember standing near the kitchen counter when I proclaimed to myself that I didn't want to be financially dependent on anyone.

My mother started seeing psychiatrists and being treated for migraine headaches. We spent many hours in pharmacies waiting for prescriptions to be filled. For various reasons, we spent time at Mom's friend's houses or shopping. When we were at home, she spent much of the time in bed sleeping. I believed I watched over my younger brother much of the time.

One day, my mother picked me up early from junior high school. She had left my father. We were going to stay at a relative's house. I felt nervous, even anxious, not knowing what he might do. He used to tell us he would haunt us in our graves. She was scared too. At the same time, I was the happiest girl alive.

We moved in with my Mom's cousin. After living at the relatives for a while, we got an apartment. We moved again twice during the next year. Our lives and what was left of the family unit were quickly crumbling. I started dating boys. My mother started going out with the girls and I would stay home and watch the kids. Our cat became really sick going to the bathroom everywhere. I tattled and said my brother was feeding the cat drugs. My mother ordered my brother and I to kill the cat. We drove to the dump, put the cat in a box and put the exhaust into the box and waited for the cat to die. We threw the box and the cat onto the trash pile and drove back home.

Mom announced one day we were moving again to another town closer to where she worked. We did not want to move again. We moved anyway. She continued to go out with the girls and she started dating. One of the men she dated showed up one day saying he had come to pick me up and we were going to meet her. I went, believing. As he drove it was obvious we were not meeting my mother. When I questioned him, he said we were going for a ride. I panicked. I know I cried. I started hollering, screaming, and begging him to take me home. But for the grace of God he did. I told my mother about it.

It was the second half of my freshman year and first half of my sophomore year in high school while we lived in this town. I didn't smoke cigarettes or pot and I hung a sign in my bedroom that said 'Get High on Life'. I had my appendix out during the summer. While recovering, I spent hours reading. Mom bought me paperbacks from the store down the street.

My mother introduced me to Al-Ateen while we lived in this foreign town. I remember talking one on one with an adult;

I thought the person was a counselor, but I'm not sure. She asked me how I was feeling. I told her I was good, but all I did was cry. This was another knock on my door from God, but my crying was too loud. I didn't know how to express my emotions.

I was scared of drinking and becoming an alcoholic, but I did experiment a few times. I went on a double date with another couple. I got so drunk on whiskey I've never drank it again in my entire life. Another boyfriend was mixing my drinks at a party. I only remember having one drink. It was my first blackout and it terrified me. I remember an image under a bridge and I remember falling out of a bed. The next day I limped when I walked. I have no memory of the rest of the night other than from other people sharing events. Looking back, I speculated if there was more than alcohol in the drink.

My boyfriend and I went out with another couple one night. We didn't come home. We got scared we would get in trouble, so we decided to run away. We developed this big plan to get some things from her house and we were leaving the state. We got caught. I was restricted from seeing her, but I was still allowed to see him.

I ran away again with this boyfriend. He found us another place to go on the outskirts of town. We stayed at a screened in gazebo at one of his friend's house. I got sick. He brought me medicine trying to heal me, but I got worse. He finally brought me to another friend's house and we turned ourselves in. From that point on I was not allowed to see him. Even though a whole bunch of these choices were wrong, I interpreted his attention as love and caring. Somebody loved me. Not being able to see him was a great loss for me.

Not too long after that, my mother drove me to my father's to live. I cried. I begged. I said, "You know how much I hate him." She dropped me off at his house; she said I was unmanageable and left. I didn't see or hear from her again for a couple of years.

While living with my father, my boyfriend came to visit. My father told him he was not allowed on the property or to see me. My father told me he contacted the school and they were directed to call the cops if I didn't show up to school. Afterwards, I devised a way for us to talk on the phone at my aunt's house. My father picked me up that afternoon and on the way home he hit me multiple times in the face and head with his right hand while he was driving. He wore a large ring on that hand and it left many large bruises. It took a couple of weeks for the black eye to heal.

From that point on I did everything in my power to not get beaten again. In order to protect myself, I became a fraud. I felt I hated him, but I would smile and act like everything was okay. Outwardly, I appeared overly responsible and was referred to as a 'goody two shoes'. I got my first job that wasn't a babysitting job. I started smoking pot and experimenting with drugs. I would say I was going bowling, but I would go to a party. I was biding my time trying to make it to the age of 18 so I could leave.

My grandfather on my father's side was having health issues and came to live with my father for a short period of time. He and my father argued a lot. Grandpa was so unhappy he called a cab one day and the cab drove him back home. Not long after that he shot himself in his own home. It was devastating knowing our grandfather committed suicide. I also lost two cousins while I was in my teens. One of them was killed in a car accident and the other was accidentally shot.

On another website, The Academy of American Physicians, it said that witnessing partner abuse can undermine children's sense of self-esteem and their confidence in the future. School-aged children are more likely to experience guilt and shame about the abuse, and they tend to blame themselves. Adolescent witnesses have higher rates of interpersonal problems with other family members, especially interparental (parent-child) conflict. They are more likely to have a fatalistic view of the future resulting in an increased rate of risk taking and antisocial behavior, such as school truancy, early sexual activity, substance abuse, and delinquency.

I graduated from high school a year early so I could leave my father's house. I had my driver's license and took my final English class at night. I put in all these extra efforts to leave, but I stayed at my father's house for another year. I was never beaten again."

*M*ore freshly brewed coffee lured two of the people from the front row to the back of the room. She watched a young woman return to her seat as she reached for her water. Chairs scraped on the floor as people got seated and settled. A couple of smoker's were returning from outside. A combination of fresh air and cigarette smoke swirled her way with the movement in the room. She stepped out from behind the podium. All of the eyes in the room followed her as she walked along the outside aisle as far as the second row of chairs.

"Some of you look the age to have lived in the seventies during the muscle car era. We had a group of teenagers that congregated in the lower parking lot of the local store where I worked. The guys drove Camaros, GTOs, Mustangs and Challengers with four-barrels, jacked up in the back with fat tires. I lived close enough to walk, but someone always gave me a ride. We acted like nosey neighbors with the cars backed in so we could see who drove by. We parked side by side with the windows open so we could talk back and forth. This was our form of social media. We'd sit for a while and then we'd cruise to the towns either north or south of us. Each town was about fifteen minutes away. Occasionally, guys from other towns would stop to visit. One guy had a two seated Datsun 240Z which didn't fit in with all these power machines. Reminds me of the movie The Fast and the Furious when Dom reveals his father's muscle car.

One day I asked one of the guys to let me drive his car. He said yes. Even with the seat all the way forward so I could reach, I didn't have the strength to push in the clutch. In order to see over the dash I sat on the edge of the seat. He let me drive slowly through town until we got to the turn-around by the railroad. Not only was I too short, I was laughing so hard I couldn't focus. He took back the wheel. I asked this same friend of mine to cut 360's in the middle of the highway after a fresh, light snow. He'd pull the emergency break, spinning us round and round like a ride at the fair. I loved the exhilaration and the thrill of the danger.

Before I reached my teens I made bold statements about going to college. During this muscle car era, I'm at the age to make it happen. What did I want to do? Who did I want to be? I had a passion for art, so I asked a local artist to take me to his college. He explained college life and introduced me to his friend who painted abstracts. I didn't know what I wanted to do; I didn't believe artists made much money and I didn't sign up. After going on a blind date that my cousin set up, I had another new boyfriend. He became my focus. We dated for six to eight months before he asked me to travel with him to another state. My gut said no to living with him, but my adventurous side wanted to see other places, other cities, and other people. He was my ticket out of town. The desire to explore justified any doubt about living with this man. I switched my thinking: I wanted to live some life before going to college. One month before I turned eighteen, I drove away in that Datsun 240Z heading to another state.

She smiled and leaned closer to the man sitting on the end of the third row and said, "You all know what life I wanted to live: I wanted to party! There were about a dozen of us traveling to this new location. The guys were millwrights with union books looking to make big bucks working shutdowns. The women stayed home and kept house. I didn't have God in my life and I didn't know living out of wed-lock was not acceptable in His eyes. I convinced myself that it was okay to use marijuana; I was still scared I'd become an alcoholic if I drank.

For the first few months while I was away, I talked to my father weekly. As time went on the calls were made less often. He would be mad at me for missing a week, which made me mad. I felt he was trying to control me. I allowed my feelings of resentment and dislike towards him surface, but I didn't express these feelings openly to him. I conveyed this message with indifference. He couldn't touch me fifteen hundred miles away.

By the fall of the same year we were back home. We rented an apartment with one of his sisters. She and I got jobs at a local manufacturing plant. We would have double-decker parties with the couple who lived below us. As the parties progressed, so did the violence. Word traveled fast at one event that people were carrying guns. After I got into a fight with a really tall girl, I hid myself in the bushes on the edge of the driveway. I did some deep soul searching. I felt totally alone. I was reliving the feelings of that little girl on the playground in third grade. This is not how I wanted to live my life."

She continued walking towards the back of the room. A few of the people turned in their chairs. She leaned against the back table and stared at the poster of the 12 Steps hanging in front of her. She reached over and picked up one of the books being offered and set it back down. She hesitated for a few seconds before she began again.

"God extends His hand and heart to us in many different ways. Bob Dylan was coming to a nearby city and a group of us bought tickets. Dylan recovered from his accident so grateful to God with his voice intact; he was promoting his new album *Saved*. I didn't want to hear his religious music; I wanted to hear those controversial, pot smoking songs. But he didn't sing any of the older songs; so we walked out. Later, secretly, I bought the album, but God still didn't have my heart.

My mother started contacting me. I would agree to meet her at a specific time, but wouldn't show. If I knew she was stopping by my apartment, I wouldn't be home. Our first meeting finally occurred and I found out she was living with a man four states away. Letting her back in my life was a slow process. She explained to me she didn't see any other choice but the one she made. I didn't tell her I saw other choices. I didn't tell her how much I missed her; how I longed for her to contact me. I didn't tell her I bought her a Christmas present, believing she'd visit me. I didn't tell her how hard I cried when I threw the gift in the trash on January first. I didn't tell her how that hurt hardened into anger."

She walked down the middle aisle back to the front for a drink of water. She grabbed both sides of the platform in front of her leaning forward. Three new people entered the room, searching for three empty chairs together. They mouthed the word sorry as they tried to be quiet as they took their seats. The room filled with the noise of wooden chairs being scraped across wooden floors as the listeners made room for the new comers.

"After work one day, my boyfriend's sister asked me if I wanted to go to college for computers. I said, "Sure." We applied and got accepted. We added another sister to the housing arrangement and moved to a bigger place. The three of us girls worked a full time job while two of us went to college. Our partying days became less and less, with most of the time consumed with work, school and studying. This went on for two years until we graduated with an Associate's degree.

After graduation, I accompanied my boyfriend to a shutdown job in the eastern side of the state. We tented in a nearby camping area. I was bored to tears and couldn't wait to get to work. I got my first job that fall. Within a few months, I got my first apartment, leaving the man I had lived with for three years.

I started seeing another employee, but we had to sneak. Company policy said employees couldn't date. After a few months of sneaking he broke up with me. He was worried about losing his job. I was crushed. I didn't understand why he wanted to keep me a secret; why didn't he want to profess his love for me? I was hurt and angry, but since I didn't know how to express emotions, I went out partying with his sister. A few months later he wanted to see me again. We got back together. I transferred to another shift. Our life outside of work consisted of drinking, golf, smoking pot, bowling, bars, dancing and our favorite video game Pac Man. I still wasn't aware of God or His commandments.

My career advanced as I progressed through various job functions. I was feeling pretty pompous; I saw an ad for a computer operator in a town forty five minutes away. The computer was an older model than the one I was currently running. I applied. During the interview, I learned the company was planning a conversion to new technology. They offered me the job with a substantial raise. After a discussion with my boyfriend, I accepted the offer.

With an abundance of money, I initiated discussions with my boyfriend about buying a house. He was open to the idea, but he was attached to the city where he grew up. We bought a home on the other side of the river. At this point, I begged him to marry me. He said he was scared of divorce, so I assured him it wasn't going to happen. We eloped. My co-workers thought I was pregnant. It must have been a long pregnancy because our first son wasn't born until two years later.

Shortly after I stopped nursing, I was extremely anxious to get back to my pot smoking. I tucked my son into bed and met my sister-in-laws out in the back yard. While we were smoking, a very loud voice said silently to me, "What are you doing?" I believe the voice was God. I did my second batch of soul searching; I didn't want my kids to have a drug addict mother. I wasn't going to raise them in the same environment I was raised. I listened to God and I quit.

I excelled in my new job as we took the company through the conversion. When I delivered reports to the senior programmers, I asked thousands of questions with the desire to become a programmer myself. As my career moved ahead, my marriage slid backward. We had a second child. Taking on the responsibilities of the children, the household and the finances exhausted me. Not knowing how to ask for help or how to address these issues, I decided the answer was to sell the house and move closer to my work. He wasn't open to the suggestion. A few months later I asked him to move out. I told him felt I was carrying the load of responsibility alone, so I might as well do it alone. While I felt confident about this decision, I was starting to be ashamed that I had lived with two men before the age of thirty. My vision for a normal life was a lifelong husband, a family, college, a good job, a house and two cats in the yard. My white picket fence fantasy was slowly being shattered.

While we were trying to sell the house, my father quit drinking. A doctor told him on two different occasions that he would die if he continued. He and I developed a new connection and started spending time together. He came to my house and played in the pool like he was a kid again. The boys and I met him at some of his fishing holes where he would fix us hotdogs off the tailgate of his truck. I came home one day to a tilled garden and a wooden sign that said happy birthday."

She glanced around the room for a clock because she didn't wear a watch. The facilitator had scheduled a ten minute break halfway through the meeting. Not finding one, she scanned the wrists of the people in the front row. A man sitting with his legs crossed and an arm draped over the top leg was wearing one. She walked up to the man, leaned over and read his watch. She had a few more minutes. Since she knew about the break ahead of time, she felt comfortable finishing the bottle of water. She smiled at the man and said, "Thank you, sir."

"One of the programmers and I had a common interest of photography. We talked frequently on the subject. He asked me to go shooting with him. We were already friends at work, so photography expanded our friendship. With the proceeds from the divorce, I bought a house. I wanted so badly to experience a happy home; I kept trying to create it. Our friendship grew and I asked him to move in with us.

Our work sent us to a drug awareness class and I realized my mother was a drug addict. Less than a year later, I got a call from her boyfriend letting me know she was in the hospital. Her addiction to prescription drugs controlled her life and was killing her. I went to hospital finding her skin and bones at 80 pounds. They kept asking me if she drank and refused to acknowledge the prescription drug issue. Her boyfriend took bottles of pills in multiple brown paper bags to the hospital, but they still insisted she drank. She stayed in a mental hospital for a month before they let her out on her own. She came to live with me. Her boyfriend refused to take her back.

She wouldn't shower or take care of her hygiene. She said she was scared of water. She went through a bottle of Tylenol a week. She was too weak to climb stairs, so she slept in the living room. All she did was sleep. I didn't understand any of this behavior. I didn't know how sick she was. I was firm that my kids were not going to be raised in the same environment I was raised in. She hadn't been there quite six months and I asked her to find another place to live. She went to live in her ex-boyfriends camp. Another friend of hers checked in on her and drove her around. She got into counseling.

My older son loved horses, so I introduced riding lessons to him. I remember being surprised that you could tell horses what to do. I took lessons too, finding my new external happiness. My boyfriend bought a thirty five acre property and we rented out my house. We camped, we hiked, we photographed, we moved, we built barns and pastures; we bought horses, horse trailers, trucks and campers. I asked my mother to come back and live with me. I became president of the horse club where my son competed.

Others were envious of my life. Externally it appeared I was living the life I dreamed of as a child. It appeared my boyfriend and I managed our relationship well, but I still wasn't happy. I had a hole in my soul. I didn't know I was spiritually and emotionally sick. I didn't have God in my life. I didn't get it when I was told I was selfish. I felt I set goals to grow in my profession, I thought I knew how to love and raise my boys, but I didn't know how to be in a relationship. A relationship was my solution, but also my problem. So I thought. We stopped talking. One hot summer day after working on the fence, I announced I wanted out of the relationship.

Within six months, I was with another new man. I set some boundaries this time. I told him I wasn't living with him unless marriage entered the discussion. We didn't stay over to each other's homes. He set his own boundary with me; he wanted to get his son to graduation. We dated for a few months, but he said he was uncomfortable with my insecurities. I blamed my bizarre behavior on growing up in domestic violence. One spring, he stopped calling me. I didn't understand the rejection, so I called him demanding to know what's going on. He blew me off. I was devastated. At this point in my life I start thinking I am the problem.

Later that fall, he calls me. I rationalize this as a sign he loves me and I'm sure we will get married. During this rekindled relationship, I learn my father has leukemia. I get into a huge argument with my father while he is in the hospital. I loudly express to my father all the anger and resentment I carried around for years. I storm out. I came home from work one day to a pile of items stacked in my driveway. Bewildered, I get out of my car and realize it was the things I had stored in my father's attic. He never spoke to me again.

A short time later, I learn through the grapevine that my father was on life support. I'm heading out of town to a training course, so I stop by to see him. I hold his hand, I tell him I love him and I cry. It was a Sunday. It was like he was waiting for me, because he died the next day. I didn't come home from my training course to go to the funeral. I wrote a letter to my brother asking him to read it at the service. The letter was all about me, comparing my computer occupation to my father's television repair business. My mother and my son's father took my sons to their grandfather's service.

God tried to contact me a couple more times. When I got home from the training class, I went to an Al-Anon meeting for some help. I was sure I was good to go with a few tools under my belt after a dozen or so meetings. Every year my boyfriend watched the Ten Commandments movie and he asked me to join him. I was only going through motions; more in seeking relief from the stress other people caused me, than admitting I had a problem. However, a seed was planted.

My father always said he was going to haunt us after he was gone and he died without a will. I didn't intend to take anything of my father's, but my selfish, superior nature decided a third of it was mine. I got into a gigantic fight with my two brothers. They called the cops on me; I disowned them. My mother and I stopped talking. I hired a lawyer, became the executor, divided the inventory and we went our separate ways. I gave away a brand new vehicle and created a joint bank account with my boyfriend. When I realized the balance in the account was shrinking, I ended the relationship with this man, swallowing my pride and walking away with my tale between my legs. I was left without any functioning relationship with any family members except my sons."

Whispers and shuffling of items near the coffee machine were getting louder. The majority of the people in the room turn as she looks in that direction. Her stomach growled as she saw someone graciously spreading out snacks.

"We will be breaking in just a few minutes so you can stretch your legs and get a snack. If I could have just a few more minutes of your attention."

The room turns back to the front as she continues her story.

"A friend asks me to go to church with her when I find myself completely alone one holiday. I went back once or twice, because I experienced peace and love while I was there. However, a few weeks later, another friend of mine introduced me to another new man. He was handsome, he was interesting, he was responsible and I believed he was the one for me. He told me his grandmother had a saying, "When you know, you know." We got married. Our blended family came together like a match made in heaven. We had the sense to get some pre-marital advice from the pastor who agreed to marry us. He had two children, I had two children; we buy a house with four bedrooms. His children came on weekends. We introduced him to camping; we bought a camper. We built a garage, we bought more land, and we built a barn. He started his own business.

My insanity affected everyone around me. I got high with the newness of the relationship. I loved making adjustments in housing, furniture and vehicles. Creating family traditions helped me feel like I belonged. However, I didn't know what to do when conflict appeared. When the going got tough, I didn't know what to say or do. I would concede and take the blame. I would blame. I would slide in and out of neurotic behavior. In the book *The Road Less Traveled* Scott Peck writes, "The neurotic assumes too much responsibility; the person with a character disorder not enough. When neurotics are in conflict with the world, they automatically assume that they are at fault. When those with character disorders are in conflict with the world, the automatically assume the world is at fault."

Our marriage was tested with our blended family. My relationship with my step-son degraded. He had tons of complications in his life starting from birth and I didn't deal with them very well at all. Without turning to God, but taking matters into my own hands, I became someone I'm not proud of. I was told I emotionally abused this child. I was told I was selfish and without compassion. I was told I was obsessed with my step-son's behavior trying to force changes. It took God to show me I entered the repeat cycle of domestic violence.

I was emotionally drained, so I found refuge in college. My professor was impressed with my first photography portfolio. I learn about the life of Jesus in my art history classes. I step back into the halls of Al-Anon for a few weeks. Additionally, I bought some business sized cards with scripture on them. The verses were specific to emotions such as anger, resentment, depression, being grateful and love. A new song by Keith Urban, *Making Memories of Us*, came on the radio which I made believe God was singing to me.

I've kept a journal for forever it seems. I picked one up a few weeks ago, coincidently opening it to the page where life was the most complicated during my marriage. At the time, I didn't feel I was connected with God; I felt like a total failure. The words written almost ten years ago referred to God. The message the words revealed was a reliance on Him, that He would guide my way.

There were four of us living together, but isolated in different sections of the house. The conversations always went sour, so we didn't talk much at all. My photographs were rich with a stillness and tranquility. I captured on film the inner peace I was seeking. A year after my youngest son left for college, I left my husband.

Even though I believed my husband was the love of my life, and even though I fully intended to reunite with him, I immediately jumped into another relationship. Very colorfully, this new man tells me I need professional help; which takes us back to June 2, 2009. On that evening, I entered into the halls of Al-Anon dedicated to recovery. God sees I'm doing some struggling in these meetings, so He sends a messenger who introduces me to the Big Book of Alcoholics Anonymous. The messenger becomes my sponsor who leads me through the 12 Steps."

The facilitator walks to the front and stands beside Leanne. He looks at her and then back at the audience. "Thank you, Leanne. We're taking a ten minute break. Those that smoke need to make sure they go to the designated area. We have more coffee brewing and assortments of snacks are on the back table. Leanne will continue promptly in ten minutes."

*A*fter the facilitator announced the meetings restart, the chatter around the snack table quieted. The noise shifted to the shuffling sounds of shoes making their way to their seats. As people got reseated, scuffing their chairs across the floor, someone in the next room dropped a pan. In unison, everyone froze, looking in the direction of the snack area. A person close-by went to offer assistance. A wave and a smile from the guilty party let the room know everything was alright. She waited at the front of the room with the facilitator as a group of smokers took their seats.

"Would everyone please get settled as Leanne continues her message?" He said. He looks at Leanne and says, "The floor is yours."

"Thank you."

She looked at the faces in the room staring back at her. "Did anyone try those homemade raspberry pastries?" She closed her eyes and kissed her fingers like the Italian cooks do, throwing her fingers into the air. Verbal confirmations came with smiles and head nods. "To whoever made those, they were delicious."

"As you heard before our break, I was the perfect example of insanity. I did the same things over and over, expecting different results. I was like the jay walker. I'd get a new boyfriend, buy all kinds of things, settle in, conflict would arise and I'd run. When I entered recovery, I thought I was getting fixed; like a mechanic fixes a car. Al-Anon was my new self help book. Secretly, I was also clinging onto the last thread of hope that if I changed, someone might love me. Compare this behavior to my childhood thinking; if I didn't rock the boat I wouldn't get beaten. My childhood behaviors were not working in my adult world.

The Fifth Tradition of Al-Anon reads like this: Each Al-Anon Family Group has but one purpose: to help families of alcoholics. We do this by practicing the Twelve Steps of AA ourselves, by encouraging and understanding our alcoholic relatives, and by welcoming and giving comfort to families of alcoholics. The Big Book of Alcoholics Anonymous is not used in Al-Anon meetings. When I tell people God brought me to a 12 Step program, they assume I am an Alcoholic. I lived in my own denial when I was using pot; I didn't see it as an addiction. I am so grateful that I listened to God's voice telling me to quit smoking pot shortly after my first son was born. My children were not exposed to drinking or drugs.

The meeting I was introduced to believe the disease of alcoholism is a family disease. Instead of separating into two different rooms, alcoholics and al-anons joined together in the same room. The meetings were open to all types of addiction. This program works for anyone who admits that their lives have become unmanageable and are willing to accept help. This program is a spiritual program meant to connect us with God. This program gets us out of the way so we can open the door and let God in.

I was quiet as I sat through my first 12 Step meeting with my sponsor. I didn't know how to express my feelings. These recovery veterans were peaceful, supportive and loving. The following sentences were read from the Big Book of Alcoholics Anonymous (Third Edition) at the opening of every meeting: The tremendous fact for every one of us is that we have discovered a common solution. We have a way out on which we can absolutely agree, and upon which we can join in brotherly and harmonious action. (Chapter 2, pg 17) We were in a position where life was becoming impossible, and if we had passed into the region from which there is no return through human aid, we had but two alternatives: one was to go on to the bitter end, blotting out the consciousness of our intolerable situation as best we could; and the other to accept spiritual help. This we did because we honestly wanted to, and were willing to make the effort. (Chapter 2, pg 25-26) We hope that no one will consider these self-revealing accounts in bad taste. Our hope is that many alcoholic men and women, desperately in need, will see these pages, and we believe that it is only by fully disclosing ourselves and our problems that they will be persuaded to say, "Yes, I am one of them too; I must have this thing." (Chapter 2, pg 29)

With my bubble burst and the wind out of my sails, I pulled my head out of the sand. God was getting my attention through these people. Spiritual help was offered long ago, in Jeremiah 31:3-4, the Lord appeared to him from afar. I have loved you with an everlasting love; therefore I have continued my faithfulness to you. Again I will build you, and you shall be built, O virgin Israel! Again you shall adorn yourself with timbrels, and shall go forth in the dance of the merrymakers.' I was looking for happiness externally through my relationships, through my work and though approval from others. My life was so wrapped up in the men of my life, that I created a timeline and based my life off which man I was with.

I wanted the burden lifted; I wanted to dance merrily. I wanted that peace and serenity I longed for as a child. I learned in Matthew 7:7-8, 'Ask and it will be given you: seek, and you will find; knock, and it will be opened to you. For every one who asks receives, and he who seeks finds, and to him who knocks it will be opened.'

These meetings were open to all types of addictions. Replace the word alcohol in the book with whatever drug you choose; replace the word alcohol with whatever you find yourself chasing. Ask yourself if any of these idols are managing your life: alcohol, food, drugs, work, money, sex, love, religion, other people, photography, video games, music, computers or sports. What is your focus? Whatever is getting your attention is the solution, not the problem. I hid behind these things in denial; I lived in a fantasy world, believing it was real. We disillusion ourselves. We are deceptive with ourselves. I spent my life being a victim of abuse. More and more people got added to my pile of rubble. Not only did I leave these men, I also left the friends and family connections created as part of being with these men.

Proverbs 28:26 says, he who trusts in his own mind is a fool; but he who walks in wisdom will be delivered. I found myself repeating my old pattern as I walked away from my 2nd husband and into another relationship. I told my husband I was leaving for selfish reasons; leaving the complex situation would benefit me. We had been struggling for three years with money, an affair and a troubled child. I was going through peri-menopause and the oldest was leaving for college. What was the real truth about us? We had no idea. I couldn't differentiate the truth from the false. I believed I was in complete control of my life and my circumstances. I believed the other people in my life needed to change to make my life better. Matthew 7:3 says it the best: 'Why do you see the speck that is in your brother's eye, but do not notice the log that is in your own eye?'

In Step 1 – We admitted we were powerless over alcohol – that our lives had become unmanageable. The biblical verse Romans 7:17: 'So then it is no longer I that do it, but sin which dwells within me.'

I spent forty years of my life chasing the peace and serenity I dreamed about as a child through external people, places and things. My way didn't work. I raised my white flag. I surrendered. I admitted defeat. I was powerless over everything. Just like Bill, I admitted I was nothing; that without Him I was lost.

"The surrender a person expresses in Step 1 rolls over into being willing in Step 2. When I reached this step, I did not believe, but I was willing to do whatever was necessary to find sanity. I knew the actions I had taken so far had not worked. The Power greater than myself in this step started out as my sponsor. I was seeking the love and peace I recognized within her soul. Each time we got together she very clearly stated she was a channel for God. She set her boundaries with me. She allowed His work to flow through her. She guided me to connect with Him.

We worked out of the Big Book of Alcoholics Anonymous and I was told to put myself into the book. I was told to replace the word alcohol with the name of my drug. Since relationships were my drug, she suggested no relationship for at least a year. For anyone going through personal growth it is suggested to not get into a new relationship.

I made it nine months and then re-entered the last broken relationship. I hadn't totally surrendered; I was lying to myself and others. My mission had been to correct my issues and reunite with my last boyfriend. I saw my actions through Bill and the jay walker; seeking love from others was my master. I compared my actions to those who are forced into recovery by a job or by the legal system. We do it to save ourselves from that moment."

She noticed the couple that was sitting next to the exit was now sitting half way down the middle aisle. They had eliminated the extra chair between them, and he was leaning her way as she whispered into his ear. The smokers occupied the seats next to the exit. The clean-up crew turned off the kitchen lights as they entered the meeting. We are such creatures of habit; the majority of the group had returned to the same seats.

"I grew up having to rely on myself as well as being the strength for my mother. I didn't grow up believing in God, didn't have a religious family and I had issues with attachment. I was a tough, tom boy and I didn't believe I needed anyone. I didn't cry and no one could hurt me. I went out into the world very head strong; full of anger. I felt I was always fighting; not only with others, but within myself. People interpreted my independence and aggression as having it all together. People admired me for my boldness. They didn't know my public character covered up my bleeding heart I had inside. I didn't know I was protecting a lonely, fearful child.

I was humbled with this step; I had to give up the fight. I had to give up the idols that I was using as my God. I had to trust and be open to a different point of view. For those having trouble giving up the fight or being willing to trust in a Higher Power ask God for the freedom to shift your thinking. Ask Him to alter your perception of a Power greater than ourselves. Some people may see God as mean; punishing, unavailable, unforgiving or that He's hateful. This same thinking got us into trouble in the first place. By revising our vision our Higher Power appears loving, tolerant, all powerful, trusting, kind, patient, accepting and forgiving.

After our friend is told by the doctor in the Big Book of Alcoholics Anonymous that he has a mind of a chronic alcoholic and that the doctor had never seen one single case recover, our friend asks, 'Is there no exception?' The doctor replies, 'Yes, there is. Exceptions to cases such as yours have been occurring since early times. Here and there, once in a while, alcoholics have had what are called vital spiritual experiences. To me these occurrences are phenomena. They appear to be in the nature of huge emotional displacements and rearrangements. Ideas, emotions, and attitudes which were once the guiding forces of the lives of these men are suddenly cast to one side, and a completely new set of conceptions and motives begin to dominate them.'

In John 14:6, Jesus said to him, 'I am the way, the truth, and the life. No one comes to the Father, but by me.' Also in John 8:12, Again Jesus spoke to them, saying 'I am the light of the world. He who follows me will not walk in darkness, but will have the light of life. Mark 11:24 states, 'Therefore I tell you, whatever you ask in prayer, believe that you received it, and it will be yours.

In Step 2 we came to believe in a Power greater than ourselves could restore us to sanity alongside the bible verse Philippians 2:13, for God is at work in you, both to will and to work for his good pleasure. These are the promises, the miracles, which each and every one of us can experience. Bill expressed in italics in his story that it was only a matter of being willing to believe in a Power greater than himself. Nothing more was required of him to make his beginning.

"*W*e've admitted we were powerless, we've become willing and now we have to make a decision. In Step 3 we make a decision to turn our will and our lives over to the care of God as we understood Him. The biblical verse says in Romans 12:1, I appeal to you therefore, brethren, by the mercies of God, to present your bodies as living sacrifice, holy and acceptable to God, which is your spiritual worship. Also consider James 1:5, If any of you lacks wisdom, let him ask God who gives to all men generously and without reproaching, and it will be given him.

The 12 Step meeting that I attended practiced a group prayer whenever a new comer reached Step 3. I was finishing Step 2, not literally at Step 3 yet, but I was at the meeting when another attendee read their third step prayer with everyone present. I believe this was my true third step as well, even though I was only a supporting participant, because of the powerful presence of the Holy Spirit I experienced.

We all got on our knees in a circle. We held hands or made sure we were touching each other in some manner so the circle was closed. The person who is reading the prayer has the book in front of them and when they are ready they read: "God, I offer myself to Thee – to build with me and to do with me as

Thou wilt. Relieve me of the bondage of self, that I may better do Thy will. Take away my difficulties, that victory over them may bear witness to those I would help of Thy power, Thy love, and Thy way of life. May I do Thy will always!" (Alcoholics Anonymous, p. 63)

As we come to believe, we also come to believe in the power of group prayer. We are told in recovery and in the bible that we are a channel for God; it is no longer about us. We are His children here on earth to do His work. This first experience of Step 3 left me and others weeping as the Holy Spirit traveled through the ring of people. There was no thunder and lightning as some describe, but an abundance of love, peace, and fulfillment. In John 3:3, Jesus answered him, 'Truly, truly I say to you, unless one is born anew, he cannot see the Kingdom of God.'

When we first reach this step, we are deciding to turn the confusion, the chaos, the misery, the unmanageability, the drinking or drugs and the dysfunction of our lives over to a Higher Power. Past experiences are different for all of us, but the common thread is insanity. If we have entered into a 12 Step program, you can be assured that we have lost our friends and families, sometimes our jobs and a place to live. You can also be assured that we are unhappy and lonely and have given up hope.

We decide to give up the fight. Imagine yourself outside in the wind. It is a constant fight to stand upright; literally leaning into the wind to walk forward. The wind catches on your clothing and sends you off in a direction you didn't intend to go. Muscles strain when you open a door to the house or the car against the wind. We have no control. Nature controls us. Now picture yourself getting inside the house or the car where there is no more fight with the wind. There's a pause, then a sigh of relief.

It is a decision. We decide to eat. We decide to sleep. We decide to drive our cars. We decide to work. Revelation 3:20 states, 'Behold, I stand at the door and knock. If anyone hears my voice and opens the door, I will come in to him and eat with him, and he with me.' We decide to answer the door."

A loud crack breaks the silence when one of the smoker's lighter hits the floor. As the owner bends over to pick up the lighter another thump follows. The person slides back their chair, scoops the bundle off the floor and bolts out the door. Another person from that group walks to the table to get another coffee. She takes a sip of water.

"That was perfect timing." She smiled.

"I really didn't know God or Jesus at this point in my life, but He knew me. Based on what I saw in others who had been through this process, I believed a Higher Power of some nature was at work in them and I was willing to have the same work done with me. Finally, I was knocking on God's door by admitting I had a problem and by being willing to do something about it. I've shared with you different events where God called me, but I couldn't hear Him because I had too much noise going on in my head. I was so headstrong, with no foresight or peripheral vision; I kept doing the same things over and over and over again. I lived in denial. I was standing in my own way.

My motto to life before recovery was wrapped up in this one phrase: If I don't make it happen, it doesn't happen. I was the judge, jury and executioner. My sponsor suggested I re-evaluate my thinking. Playing God was not working. I needed to turn my life over to a Higher Power. In Ezekiel 11:19 it states, 'And I will give them one heart, and put a new spirit within them; and I will take the stony heart out of their flesh and give them a heart of flesh.'

I was so busy searching for someone to take care of me; I didn't know how to take care of myself. While God was converting me, one of the things I did was create mini posters and leave notes to myself. One of them said: God Please keep me divorced from self-pity, dishonesty and self-seeking motives. I kept this in my kitchen so I could see it as I went to and fro. I found a list of promises on the internet that stated what I would be like as I recovered from codependency. I like to scrapbook so I created a scrapbook page with these promises on it and hung it in my office where I used my computer. This new thinking wasn't intuitive for me and these little reminders comforted me.

Another practice I developed was when I lay my head on my pillow at night; I would say the Lord's Prayer over and over and over again until I would wake up in the morning realizing at some point I had fallen asleep. This solution shut down the noise in my head that seemed to get louder as soon as I shut off the lights and closed my eyes.

I learned it was time to love myself. I didn't know how. A fellow recovery friend suggested I look straight into the eyes staring back at me in the mirror and say, 'I love you'. Those eyes pleaded with me to hear, 'You are so beautiful'. It felt awkward, but I did it. I trusted these people because I could see God's miracle in them. They were transformed. I needed to do something different. My old way did not work.

In 1 John 3:1-2 it states, 'see what love the Father has given us that we should be called the children of God; and so we are. The reason why the world does not know us is that it did not know him. Beloved, we are God's children now; it does not yet appear what we shall be, but we know that when he appears we shall be like him, for we shall see him as he is.

God was recreating my old self into someone new. God was driving. Allowing God to drive is either a yes or no question and I said yes while we were on our knees on the floor praying.

God

Grant me the serenity to accept the things I cannot change

The courage to change the things I can and

The wisdom to know the difference

Romans 5:2-5 states 'Through Him we have obtained access to this grace in which we stand, and we rejoice in our hope of sharing the glory of God. More than that, we rejoice in our sufferings, knowing that suffering produces endurance, and endurance produces character, and character produces hope, and hope does not disappoint us, because God's love has been poured into our hearts through the Holy Spirit which has been given to us.'"

"The Bible says in Lamentations 3:40, let us test and examine our ways, and return to the Lord. How do we do this? We entered into prayer with God in Step 3, and He will help us do Step 4 – Made a searching and fearless moral inventory of ourselves. This was not an easy thing to do because I was busy blaming others and living in denial. However, the Bible also says in Romans 8:5-8, for those who live according to the flesh set their minds on the things of the flesh, but those who live according to the Spirit set their minds on the things of the Spirit. To set the mind on the flesh is death, but to set the mind on the Spirit is life and peace. For the mind that is set on the flesh is hostile to God; it does not submit to God's law, indeed it cannot; and those are in the flesh cannot please God.

I spent the majority of my life putting myself in dysfunctional caretaker roles. The little girl inside me twisted the role of taking care of others into thinking I was being loved. I always comforted my mother after my father beat her. She would ask me to help analyze what went wrong. I would try. It made me feel good. It comforted her. I felt loved. This behavior pattern elevated me. I got high on this. I'm only five feet tall, but my pride measured out at nine feet tall. Add the ingredients of my circumstances, such as college, career, owning a home, marriage, family; I believed I was better than others. My heart was so cold; I was not approachable to those who didn't know me.

I didn't know I was covering up feelings of shame. I didn't know I had built a thick wall around the fear of being inadequate. I didn't know I was hiding and protecting a scared little girl who still lived inside me. I didn't know I was immature. I didn't know what love was. I didn't know how to love. I didn't know I was putting myself in a victim role by blaming both my mother and father for my unhappiness. I didn't know I did this same thing to the men in my life. I didn't know putting others down was a dysfunctional way to make me feel good. I didn't know these were the burdens I was carrying. I didn't know I was in jail.

Paul tells us in Romans 2:1, therefore you have no excuse, O man, whoever you are, when you judge another; for in passing judgment upon him you condemn yourself, because you, the judge, are doing the very same things. The Big Book tells us almost none of us liked the self-searching, the leveling of our pride, the confessing of shortcomings which the process requires for its successful consummation. In order to connect with God, it meant the destruction of our self-centeredness. It was time for us to learn who we really were and to own our behavior.

The process starts by being willing. I bought a notebook. I was told to write a prayer in my own handwriting at the top of each page. We continue by listing the people we are angry at, those we dislike and all the people we resent. This was such an easy section for me. My life was full of blaming others. The process works in columns. Do all of column one first, column two second and so on and so forth. My sickness found this first column fun. In the second column we list the cause of the resentment and in column 3 we list how it affected us. Our self esteem, our pocketbooks, our ambitions and our personal relations are hurt or threatened.

I'm resentful at:	The Cause	Affects my:
Last husband	His affair	Self-esteem (fear)
		Sex relations
		Security (fear)

We may have resentments against institutions or principles which get listed as well. For many years I could work myself into a rage over public bathrooms. The women's rooms might have 3 stalls. Now we all know it takes us women longer to go to the bathroom for many reasons, but the basic fact is, we sit. I found out that the men's room gets 3 stalls, PLUS one or two urinals. During the 1980's, if I went to a public function with you and if we needed to use the bathroom, I'm quite sure I went on and on about the unfairness of the bathrooms. I would get angry. I remember convincing a couple of women to join me in using the men's room on one occasion. Our group didn't get caught, but other women followed my lead and security was then posted by the men's room door.

Some people stop at this step. As I've worked with others, some aren't willing do the third step prayer. The Big Book states it is plain that a life which included deep resentment leads only to futility and unhappiness. For when harboring such feelings we shut ourselves off from the Sunlight of the Spirit. We know this through our own experience. The Bible promises in Isaiah 35:3-4, strengthen the weak hands, and make firm the feeble knees. Say to those who are of a fearful heart, "Be strong, fear not! Behold, your God will come with vengeance, with the recompense of God. He will come and save you." The Big Book also says we decided that hereafter in this drama of life; God was going to be our Director. He is the Principal; we are His agents. He is the Father, and we are His children. Most good ideas are simple, and this concept was the keystone of the new and triumphant arch through which we passed to freedom.

After the first three columns are complete, we turn the paper over and the focus is redirected onto ourselves. We are in prayer while we are doing our inventory and we ask God to show us what our role was. Was I selfish? Was I self-seeking? Was I dishonest? Was I wrong? Was I at fault? Was I to blame? Did I make a mistake in my thinking? We ask God to show us this for each cause listed for each person. Some people we listed may have many, many causes. If we are open to allowing God to show us the truth about ourselves, this is a very humbling exercise. It was very revealing to see repeated over and over how selfish and self-seeking or dishonest we were. At any point during this process if we stay focused on the people and the resentments, we have God blocked and we will not hear his answer to our question. We will not transform; we will behave the same as we always have. We will continue to carry our burdens and we will sit in jail. Our question was to have Him show us the truth about ourselves, not the truth about others. We don't have to worry if we get this right; we only have to be open to letting God show us.

We all react to the situations in our lives differently. Some people don't get angry; they say they don't have resentments.

I was the type to walk out of the house, slam the door, jump into my vehicle and screech the tires going out of the driveway. I'd talk about you and put you down for days. Others suppress their anger and withdraw. In one of our meetings a member was struggling with identifying their resentments. The person stated they didn't get angry. God helped us coach the person to tone it down and ask God to help them list people and behaviors they didn't like. God told us to tell this person that this step is about connecting with God. God spoke through us to this person that we do whatever it takes to recover from our hopeless state, because our hopeless state keeps us from God. The person came back the next week and thanked us all for taking the time for them. The person went home that night and prayed and came up with 78 resentments. We didn't do this, God did. God wants all of His children to join Him and He puts us to work, if we are willing, to make it happen.

In 2 Corinthians, 5:20 it says, so we are ambassadors for Christ, God making his appeal through us. We beseech you on behalf of Christ, be reconciled to God.

Once all our grudges are exhausted onto paper, we move on to our fears. The same column process is used. List the fears. What elicits the fear? A simple one might be spiders, but a more complicated one might be the fear of saying 'no' to people. I didn't have too many of the typical spider, snakes or the dark, but I had an abundant list regarding the inability to say 'no', someone else's anger, and being ignored or rejected. I grew up a tough little tom-boy, not afraid of anything. I made believe I wasn't afraid of my father. The last time I cried was when my mother left and when my father beat me. Listing my fears was a huge revelation for me. God showed me that all that toughness, the aggression, the anger, the caretaking; was covering up and protecting a scared little child that still lived within me. God revealed to me that I was scared that no one loved me and that I would be alone and that I'd be rejected. God held my hand while He revealed to me that I was full of shame; toxic shame. It wasn't that I had a problem; I believed I was the problem. I was shocked to count and add up almost 50 fears. Additionally, I realized that I failed myself in the area of self-reliance. I expected others to comfort me and take care of me emotionally and spiritually and when my expectations weren't met, the resentment cycle resumed. He revealed that fear was not getting what I wanted or losing what I had. I cried after realization of my fears. Day after day, night after night I cried. I would have a good day and the next day I would cry all over again. The tough outer shell of the frightened little girl was crumbling. I was all by myself for the first time in my life; the very place I had avoided. For the very first time I was feeling the childhood pain I had buried for years.

The next part of our inventory regarded sex. In column 1 we were to answer this question: Where have I been selfish, dishonest or inconsiderate? The question in column 2 was: Where did I unjustifiably arouse jealousy, suspicion, or bitterness? And the 3rd column asks: Whom have I hurt? In this section, I found I wasn't promiscuous. There was only one time I had an affair. I wasn't in a relationship, but the guy I dated was engaged to be married. I didn't consider myself a flirt but yet I knew how to charm you. I didn't think of my husband's feelings when a male co-worker picked me up in a mustang convertible and we drove off together. To me he was a work associate, but my husband was very jealous and suspicious. I also learned that I had a new man in mind as the relationship with the current man was coming to an end. What I learned about myself in the sexual arena is that I used sex to market myself. I used it to attract and I used it to keep your focus. I also used it to punish. Whom did I hurt? Each and every man I was in a relationship with. I found my sex inventory wasn't about sex. It was about my character. It was about my conduct. I wasn't taking very good care of myself in this area either. I wasn't being very nice to others. I was manipulating. 2 Corinthians 11:30 says, if I must boast, I will boast of the things that show my weakness.

The first time through a fourth step inventory we worry we didn't do it correctly or didn't uncover everything. What is important is to do this as best we can right now. The 12 Step program is a program for living; it is a process; it's a way to get ourselves and keep ourselves out of the way so we can have a relationship with God. Depending on our age when we do our fourth step, we may have many years of inventory to list. If we continue using the 12 Steps as our design for living, later on we will use the 10th step to keep our house clean and in order on a day to day basis.

While in prayer with God, this inventory identifies the characteristics of our self-will. With God's guidance and our willingness, He will remove these obstacles for us so we can do God's will. Our bodies are vessels for His Holy Spirit to work through us and bring His message to others. I spent half of my life longing for love; longing for happiness and longing for peace. I wake each morning and my first thoughts are to praise God for my new day. I thank God for providing His Son Jesus as a sacrifice and for Jesus dying on the cross for our sins. I express how grateful I am to have Him in my heart. I tell Him how gracious I am for the gifts He has given me. I believed at the start of this 12 Step process, I was entering another self-help program. I thought the action of doing my inventory granted me a new character. I know now my new character came from God. As I built a relationship with God, I thank Him for being with me before I even knew He was there. When I made the announcement that I wanted to go to college, I believe He was revealing to me the life He had laid out for me. He led me to where I am today.

Jesus states in Luke 11:9-10, And I tell you, ask and it will be given to you, seek and you will find. Knock and it will be open to you. For everyone who asks receives, and he who seeks finds, and to him who knocks it will be opened.

Each time I am aware I am edgy with others, I repeat my prayer I listed at the top of each page of my inventory: "God give me the courage, strength and perseverance to see the truth about myself so I may better do Thy will." I do this while I'm driving, while I'm in the grocery store or even as part of my job. If I'm feeling angry and resentful towards others, then something is going on with me. If I'm being judgmental or even thinking judgmental thoughts, then something is going on with me. If I've set up expectations then I've created resentments which means, something is going on with me. If I'm rolling my eyes at someone, something is going on with me. If I'm obsessed with or about something, then something is going on with me. If something is going on with me, I've lost my contact with God. If I've lost my contact with God, I've lost the love, happiness and peace. I'm not willing to lose that. I'm not willing to lose Him. He granted me my wish that I desired as a child. He granted me Grace. If something is going on with me, I only need to once again surrender, be willing and miracles happen.

In Proverbs 28:13, it states he who conceals his transgressions will not prosper, but he who confesses and forsakes them will obtain mercy."

"In Step 5 we admit to God, to ourselves and to another human being the exact nature of our wrongs. In James 5:16 it states, therefore confess your sins to one another and pray for one another that you may be healed. The prayer of a righteous man has great power in its effects.

Writing inventory is a difficult process of looking at ourselves. We do it by ourselves at the directive of God. Immediately after completing our life long list of resentments, fears and sex conduct, we meet with our sponsor and share all of it. I had a notebook full. My sponsor and I started on a Saturday morning after breakfast continuing on through the next two meals. We parted to get some rest with plans to meet again the next day. Finishing up on the second day took half as much time as the first. My sponsor kept asking me if I had anything else I wanted to share.

I was totally exhausted and drained; I said, "No."

Prior to recovery, I spent hours telling my friends about the troubles in my life. I was looking for support from my friends which I found out from my inventory that I was self seeking. I learned 'sharing my troubles' was a way of making others in my life wrong; a way of building myself up. I was humbled to realize I really was as selfish as the men in my life told me I was.

Step 5 breaks down the barriers we have erected through our addictions. These walls not only separate us from our family and friends; the biggest divide is from ourselves and our Father. Being willing to recover forces our hand with honesty; if we aren't honest, we won't recover. We will stay stuck and keep repeating the same behaviors over and over again. This is our opportunity to share our vulnerabilities; to share how it really felt when your father pulled down your pants, laid you over his knee and hit your bottom with a stick. It's a chance to let the little child inside of us describe to an adult the purple lines about an inch wide crisscrossed from our bottom down to the middle of the back of our legs. It's our time to cry because there was no other adult who stepped up to stop the abuse. It's our opening to see the connection between an adult longing for love to the child walking across the elementary school playground feeling unloved and alone. If we are honest, God's love aids us to see the protective behaviors of the past that are no longer working or necessary. For the very first time we reveal our deepest, darkest secrets to another human being. For the very first time we reveal our deepest, darkest secrets to ourselves. In Ephesians 4:14-15 it says, so that we should no longer be children, tossed to and fro and carried about with every wind of doctrine, by the cunning of men, by the craftiness in deceitful wiles, rather speaking the truth in love we are to grow up in every way into him who is the head, into Christ. Later, in Ephesians 4:25 it states, therefore, putting away falsehood, let everyone speak the truth with his neighbor, for we are members one of another.

I entered into recovery because I could no longer live the life I was living. I had reached a point where I had given up; I didn't want the internal fight to go on. I became a balloon that had lost all of its air. I was the branch of a tree that finally broke after being windblown for years. I was the dam that broke and was no longer strong enough to hold back the water. I had reached surrender. I was entirely ready to have God help me.

The Big Book gave me a fifth step promise: We pocket our pride and go to it, illuminating every twist of character, every dark cranny of the past. Once we have taken this step, withholding nothing, we are delighted. We can look the world in the eye. We can be alone at perfect peace and ease. Our fears fall from us. We begin to feel the nearness of our Creator. We may have had certain spiritual beliefs, but now we begin to have a spiritual experience. The feeling that the drink problem has disappeared will often come strongly. We feel we are on the Broad Highway, walking hand in hand with the Spirit of the Universe."

"**W**hen we reached Step 6 we were entirely ready to have God remove all these defects of character. Humble yourselves before the Lord, and he will exalt you it says in James 4:10.

If I am totally honest with myself, I can replace that word alcohol with many other words.

I can replace the word alcohol with power. I got high and experienced grandiose with the power I thought I had being the family hero. I played God.

I can replace the word alcohol with adrenaline. I had a desire to live on the edge. I would ask my guy friends to take me out during a snow storm and pull the emergency break and cut cookies in the middle of the road. I remember hanging onto an open car door during a snow storm using my feet as skis on the tar road while the driver kept right on driving. When I learned to ride a horse, I raced others to win. Racing fed the adrenaline and winning fed the power.

I can replace the word alcohol with intelligence. I had great pride in being smart. A girl friend in 5th grade said to me, "You may be smart, but I know more about boys than you do." Being intelligent brought me attention and put me into groups of other intelligent people. My intelligence also brought me power and kept me feeling 'better than' in other groups of people.

I can replace the word alcohol with love. I wanted more than anything else in the world to be loved. I became a chameleon in order to receive love. I set aside my boundaries and self reliance for love. I didn't love myself, yet I wanted love from others. I didn't know how to love people; I wanted people to love me.

I can replace the word alcohol with having to be right. I argued to be right and damaged many, many relationships with many people. Included in the list of people was my father. I believed for years that my father didn't love me. I did not and could not grasp that if someone neglected me by spending all their time drinking or being drunk that they loved me. I did not and could not believe if someone loved me they would beat me. I had trouble identifying truth from false. I was basing everything purely on my perception. It was my story. I'm not saying I agree with his behavior; however it doesn't say he didn't love me. I learned I was a very sick, dysfunctional person. I was hurting inside. Well, so was he. I didn't have the capacity or compassion to see this from any other point of view other than my own.

I can replace the word alcohol with money. I became self sufficient and fulfilled my goal as a child. I didn't want to be in the same position as my mother. However, that also raised me to a position of power and I became controlling like my father.

I can replace the word alcohol with charm. I have always been petite and slender. I like to exercise to stay healthy. I am not shy and I love to meet new people. I love to laugh and enjoy life and engage in a 'get to know you' conversation. I learned to hide behind this charm. I might be dying inside, having a really bad day, but you won't know it. I realized this made me a fraud.

I can replace the word alcohol with marijuana. For ten years of my life I didn't go without this drug. I give Him all the praise for taking the craving and obsession away. I had no desire for it at all after that evening in the back yard.

I can replace the word alcohol with the words pride, gossip, self centeredness, sarcasm, arrogance and being a chameleon. Romans 6:12 states let not sin therefore reign in your mortal bodies, to make you obey their passions.

1 Peter 1:13-16 says therefore gird up your minds, be sober, set your hope fully upon the grace that is coming to you at the revelation of Jesus Christ. As obedient children, do not be conformed to the passions of your former ignorance, but as he who called you is holy, be holy yourselves in all your conduct; since it is written, "You shall be holy, for I am holy."

Psalms 51:10 says create in me a clean heart, O God; and put a new and right spirit within me.

These behaviors are the only ones I had ever known. Could I set these aside? Could I let them go? Did I trust and believe in an unseen power greater than myself? Have I seen all of my blemishes? Can I accept these defects about myself without self-shaming?

When we do the 3rd Step prayer, we are considered 'in prayer' until we finish Step 7; humbly asked Him to remove our shortcomings. I spent the majority of my adult life reading self help books, learning about low self-esteem and insecurities with the intent to change. I was seeking happiness; I was seeking love. I would read about behaviors described as mine and I'd try to implement their solution. Within no time, I was back repeating those same behaviors I wanted to lose. I was unable to change on my own. I wasn't really sure what to expect from these 12 Steps. I only knew I saw in others a peaceful nature that I wanted to have.

1 John 1:9 says if we confess our sins, he is faithful and just and will forgive us our sins and cleanse us from all unrighteousness. I humbly asked Him to remove my shortcomings. I got down on my knees in my sponsors apartment and read the 7th Step prayer:

My Creator, I am now willing that you should have all of me, good and bad. I pray that you now remove from me every single defect of character which stands in the way of my usefulness to you and my fellows. Grant me strength, as I go out from here, to do your bidding. Amen." (Alcoholics Anonymous, p76)

"The 12 Step process continues on with Step 8 – Made a list of all persons we had harmed and became willing to make amends to them all. Luke 6:31 states and as you wish that men would do to you, do so to them. Mark 11:25 says and whenever you stand praying, forgive, if you have anything against anyone; so that your Father also who is in heaven may forgive you your trespasses. Matthew states this same thing again in 6:14-15: For if you forgive men their trespasses, your heavenly Father also will forgive you: but if you do not forgive men their trespasses, neither will your Father forgive your trespasses.

After the list is written, we move on to Step 9 – Made direct amends to such people wherever possible, except when to do so would injure them or others. Matthew 5:23-24 says so, if you are offering your gift at the altar and there remember that your brother has something against you; leave your gift there before the altar and go; first be reconciled to your brother; then come and offer your gift. In Psalms 90:17 the Bible states let the favor of the Lord our God be upon us, and establish thou the work of our hands upon us; yea, the work of our hands establish thou it.

If I said sorry to the people in my life once, I said it a thousand times; only to repeat the same offense over and over again. Additionally, I might not apologize at all; I wasn't willing to admit my wrongs. I hid behind denial which meant I didn't even know I was the one in the wrong. Even worse, I might stand with my hands on my hips, leaned a little forward, demanding an apology from you.

The resentment list from Step 4 became the list of people I had harmed for Step 8. My sponsor encouraged me to list others whom I owed amends, but may not have shown up on my list of resentments. Some people landed on my amends list because I spent an enormous amount of time badmouthing them, making them wrong, and convincing others that these people were wrong or needed help. These people on my list may not know I did this to them. She also guided me that in some cases, I may truly be the victim; such as when I was a child living in the world of domestic violence. Most important, we are NOT to make amends to anyone if it is going to injure them or cause harm.

I hadn't turned all of my shortcomings over to God as I was still learning this new way of life. My amends process wasn't very thorough. I was sincere, but the depth wasn't there. God takes care of us and only reveals what we are ready for. I made direct amends to those who were current in my life; ex-boyfriend, people at work and friends. I wrote letters to all of the prior men in my life never intending to mail any. However, I did mail one of the letters and received a letter back from that individual. He agreed with me; I had hurt him. We are taught to listen and accept comments from those we had harmed. Let them vent; ask them to share the discomfort we caused them.

Once we turn our lives over to God, He does his work. I moved to a new town. My landlord introduced me to a transformational education program that intrigued me. As she enrolled me, I compared her information to my experience with the 12 Step process. With God directing me (I was listening) and my curiosity, I registered. This was God's way of telling me I had more work to do.

We talked to total strangers sitting next to us about very humbling, sensitive experiences in our lives. We were prompted to list people who we wished we had better relations with. We learned to differentiate facts from the stories we made up in our heads. We listened and watched people transform before our eyes from an angry, non-forgiving stance to a softer, humble attitude. I learned that if I have an issue with someone, I need to look at that same issue within myself. I learned you are a mirror of me; if I call you judgmental, then I am being judgmental.

I realized that even though my mother and I had talked over our issues and difficulties we experienced in our relationship, I had never apologized to her for my behavior. I called her at our next break and told her my revelation. I apologized. She accepted. It was a powerful experience. I called each one of my sons and told them I wanted to have a conversation with them regarding my behavior as their mother. I told them repeatedly as they were growing up that alcoholism ran in our family, but I never told them that I was codependent and that runs in the family as well. As I moved in and out of relationships, I didn't take into consideration how they were affected. I would go to the school and tell the teachers what was going on in their lives, I would take their emotions into consideration, but I never stopped my repeat behavior FOR them. I realized my lack of ability to commit to men might give the young son's in my life a sense of insecurity around commitment. I opened up my soul to the both of them and made a commitment to them that I will always be there for the both of them. I made a commitment to support and assist them in whatever dreams and desires they might have. I love them and I admitted to them my selfish choices.

I called my ex-husband, the love of my life. I asked if he would meet with me so I could make amends. He agreed. The transformational program had just helped me learn that I have an overwhelming desire to be right. The life with my ex-husband flashed before my eyes; the fights and arguments, the standoff and the stale mates. The finger pointing and defending and justifying were all expressed to make sure I was right. I spent hours analyzing my step son's behavior to prove I was right and he wasn't going to outsmart me with his lies. I spent hours pointing out why I believed my husband didn't love and support me. He kept telling me I didn't have any compassion and four years later God showed me that I didn't have any compassion. I learned I was operating out of fear, but I covered the fear with aggression. I had a hole in my soul. I protected my aching heart with a sharp tongue. I may not drink, but I was practicing the same behavior that I saw my father practice. I was acting just like my father. I practiced the very behavior I didn't like practiced on me. I lost the love of my life."

The woman half of the couple leaned forward, searching through her bag. The color of her nose revealed she was searching for a tissue. His hand on her back was caressing her in a gentle, swirling motion. Finding none, she got up and went to the ladies room. The chair scraped across the floor as he realigned his chair with hers. More scuffing sounds chimed in as others did the same as she settled back into her seat stuffing a wad of tissue into her purse.

"I offered to make amends to my step-son, but he declined. I offered a second time, but he wasn't willing. I wrote and mailed letters on a couple of occasions pouring out my apologies and regrets. Not everyone we approach is open to the process. I have my step-son tucked in my prayers and have turned him over to God. He's God's child.

My father and I were not talking to each other when he passed away. While he was in the hospital being treated for leukemia, I shouted and screamed and dumped all of the anger I had bottled up inside me. I told him I didn't believe he loved me. How could he do those things he did if he loved me; if he loved us? I didn't have the capacity to separate the sin from the sinner. I admired so many things about my father, but my resentment kept me from having a relationship with him. I limited my sons relationship with him. I understand today the boundary I set for myself and for my sons was healthy due to his drinking, but I didn't keep my distance totally because of his drinking. I was mad and angry and I disliked him. I didn't want my sons to experience with him what I had experienced. Who was I to think he would behave the same way with them? Since my father is no longer here, I wrote him a letter. I know today he had a disease; he had the disease of alcoholism. He had a hole in his soul. He treated his aching heart with alcohol and he practiced domestic violence. For all I know, he didn't even remember doing it. It doesn't make it right, but as an adult I didn't need to keep playing the victim. We are all sinners. The act of forgiveness is powerful.

My father played the harmonica and loved to dance. He was a handsome man and always wore a hat. Not a baseball cap, a hat. He could draw and he would hang his work in his garage. He knew how to work on vehicles; he could do plumbing, electrical, landscaping, and photography. He built our house and garage. He would take us swimming and he would swim with us. He'd play with us. He was an outdoorsman and loved to hunt and fish. He taught us about survival in the wilderness. We didn't get too excited about it, but he taught us about gardening. He managed his money well and after I started a 401k in the working world, he and I talked about investing. Another year, he made me a huge pot of fish chowder. I was so absorbed in my self-pity; I continued to make him out as a bad guy. I put him down to make me big.

God showed me I had the same behavior; how could I do the things I did if I loved my husband; if I loved his son? I did it because I had the disease of alcoholism. I had a hole in my soul. I am a sinner. I did the best I could with what I had. My father did the best he could with what he had. My mother did the best she could. We were all broken.

In Luke 6:37-38 it states judge not, and you will not be judged; condemn not, and you will not be condemned; forgive, and you will be forgiven; give, and it will be given to you; good measure, pressed down, shaken together, running over, will be put into your lap. For the measure you give will be the measure you get back.

In 1 Peter 1:22 the Bible says having purified your souls by the obedience to the truth for a sincere love of the brethren, love one another earnestly from the heart.

I protected and shielded my sons from alcoholics, drug addicts and smokers which included most of my family. My solution was to keep them out of my life. My behavior wasn't always expressed in a loving, healthy manner. I came to believe I was better than they were. As I share my testimony with you, I am humbled that God used an alcoholic to lead me through this process. I blamed the alcoholics and drug addicts for my dysfunctional life and He used an alcoholic to lead me to Him."

She scans the room for the man with the watch; her clock. She's disappointed when she sees he's no longer in the room. She finishes her bottle of water and then walks around the podium standing beside it. She smells the aroma of another pot of fresh coffee. Looking towards the coffee pot area she sees her timekeeper.

"A while after I finished Step 12, I found myself in turmoil. My attitude was sliding and I found myself feeling those same old feelings I thought had been washed away through the cleansing when God had bathed me. I thought gone meant gone. In my human thinking, I thought once I had gone through the 12 Steps I was fixed, corrected, healed. I didn't realize that temptations would always surface and try to interfere. I turned to my sponsor with my questions; why do I feel this way and what is going on with me? She was uncertain and advised me to contact another woman for some assistance. I made an appointment to meet this person and we had a very revealing conversation.

She told me I needed to practice Step 10 – Continued to take personal inventory and when we were wrong promptly admitted it. She told me that I needed to pay attention to 1 Corinthians 10:12 which says, therefore let anyone who thinks that he stands take heed lest he fall. This person, acting as God's guide, explained to me that our fears and our character defects arise and over rule our love and connection to God if we aren't doing the work. It's a daily process to keep ourselves out of the way in order to remain connected to our Higher Power; whom I chose to call God or Jesus interchangeably. God is the only one who will provide us with grace; freely I might add. If we find that nasty old rotten self is ruling us, we are letting sin run our lives. She encouraged me to look at my fears. Fear has such a strong control over us all; we don't even realize it. As I told you earlier, I was shocked to learn about my fears. The process to see my fears was the same Step 4 method only in a slightly smaller scale. Dig out my worksheets, write some inventory and call a sponsor to share it. Oh.

Proverbs 14:14-15 says a perverse man will be filled with the fruit of his ways, and a good man with the fruit of his deeds. The simple believes everything, but the prudent looks where he is going.

I did what I was told. I found fear was the root of my issue. Through God's help I realized I used my relationships with men to hide. I used these relationships to blame. I used these relationships to look good. At this point, as I was seeking direction with my turmoil, I found I feared I would never have a functional relationship because relationships were my drug. I found I was in turmoil because I was trying to run the show. I learned that peace and serenity enter our souls when we focus on God and let Him run the show. I wasn't in a relationship, didn't know if I was ever going to have another relationship and I was creating stress within my life because of it. That is fear. Fear of being alone; fear of not being liked;

fear of being unworthy; same old fear I was introduced to a few months earlier. Once again, I needed to go back to Steps 1, 2 and 3 and surrender to God. I was trying to create my own plan…again.

I learned that I needed to go up and down these steps on a daily basis. The first three steps we make peace with God. Steps four through seven we make peace with ourselves. Steps eight, nine and ten we make peace with others. The last two steps help us keep the peace.

I called my sponsor and asked her if she would give me time so I could do another Step 5. Thank God she was willing. God revealed to me that I got so good at hiding my fear as a child; I don't recognize fear or acknowledge it when it starts growing. It's like mold. It's there before you see it.

In the Matthew 13:37-43, Jesus explains to His disciples about the parable of the weeds. The Son of Man plants the good seeds. The field is the world and the good seeds represent the Kingdom. The weeds are the people who belong to the evil one. At the end of the world the weeds will be burned and the good seeds will shine like the sun in their Father's Kingdom. I personalized it. I am God's garden. If I'm willing, He will plant good seeds in me (characteristics like Jesus) and remove the weeds (character defects). God created this 12 Step process using Bill W. and Dr. Bob in 1935 to help us weed our own gardens. Once we have our garden in good shape, we are asked to show others how to weed theirs.

In Matthew 5:8 it says blessed are the pure in heart for they shall see God. Also, in 1 John 2:15-17 the Bible says do not love the world or the things in the world. If anyone loves the world, the love for the Father is not in him. For all that is in the world – the lust of the flesh, the lust of the eyes, and the pride of life - - is not of the Father but of this world. And the world passes away, and the lust of it; but he who does the will of God abides forever.

In Proverbs 12:1 the Bible says whoever loves discipline loves knowledge, but he who hates reproof is stupid. Each day we have to weed our garden. We ask God to help us weed our garden. What are our needs? What are our feelings? What counterfeit, codependent, and addictive means are we using to meet our needs? Are we manipulating others? Do we recognize these weeds? Do we have healthy boundaries? Do we admit our wrongs promptly?

The Big Book of Alcoholics is full of promises starting on page 84 and 85 of the Third edition. Remember the fight I described to you earlier? The Big Book says we have ceased fighting anything and anyone – even alcohol. For by this time sanity will have returned. We will seldom be interested in liquor. If tempted, we recoil from it as from a hot flame. We react sanely and normally, and we will find that this has happened automatically. We will see that our new attitude toward liquor has been given us without any thought of effort on our part. It just comes. That is the miracle of it. We are not fighting it, neither are we avoiding temptation. We feel as though we had been placed in a position of neutrality – safe and protected.

I woke up one day and realized my low self-esteem, my shame, was gone. I got angry but dealt with the issue immediately speaking in a calm, even tone. It baffled me. The Big Book promised me the problem would be removed. It would not exist. The Bible promises the same thing. However, weeds can take over. The Big Book promises that this will all remain true if we keep in a fit spiritual condition. We are never cured, but we get a daily reprieve contingent on the maintenance of our spiritual condition. That's why I'm standing here talking to you today."

We have entered the World of the Spirit.
Love and tolerance of others is our code.

The 10th Step Promise – And we have ceased
fighting anything and anyone – even alcohol.
For by this time sanity will have returned.
We will seldom be interested in liquor.

Alcoholics Anonymous, pg 84

Step 10 – Continued to take personal inventory and when we were wrong promptly admitted it.

Resentments? _____

Fear? _____

Selfishness? _____

Dishonesty? _____

Who did we discuss this with? _____

With whom did we need to make amends? _____

What could we have done better? _____

What can we do for others? _____

Did my actions promote love? _____ Were my actions honest and sincere? _____

"*A*fter I finished the 12 Step process with my sponsor a very loud voice kept saying to me, "You should go to church." I heard the message, but I ignored it. The next week rolled around and the voice spoke up again. I ignored it again. Step 11 says that we sought through prayer and meditation to improve our conscious contact with God as we understood Him, praying only for knowledge of His will for us and the power to carry that out. I started questioning my disregard of this message. God was talking to me. I still didn't go to church. But this voice would not go away. In the quiet of my apartment I spoke out loud throwing my hands up into the air, "Okay, okay, I'll go to church." I went to find out who He is. I went to let the word of Christ dwell in you richly, teach and admonish one another in all wisdom, and sing psalms and hymns and spiritual songs with thankfulness in your hearts to God as it states in Colossians 3:16."

Repeating her earlier walk around the room she stopped by the second row of chairs. The gentleman with the watch automatically shows her his arm and the time as he returned to his seat in the front row. She smiles at him. He tips his head back to her.

"I started praying through the promptings of my sponsor. The first person I prayed for was my most recent ex-boyfriend.

My sponsor suggested a simple prayer seeking his happiness, health and prosperity. It didn't have too much depth and I'm not really sure how much meaning I put behind it, but I prayed for him. Each time another dramatic interaction would occur with another person, I would pray for their happiness, health and prosperity. That's it. I would say this over and over and over again to keep resentment from seeping into me. I prayed for my ex-husband, his son, his new girlfriend. I prayed for people in grocery store lines who were being impatient. I prayed for people with road rage. I prayed for my sons.

I started to notice a change in me. I wasn't so angry with my ex-boyfriend and his behaviors didn't bother me anymore. I wasn't mad at my ex-husband and saw his affair from a different angle. It was his way of dealing with stress. I'm not saying it didn't hurt, but the feelings weren't ruling me. I wasn't scared or annoyed with his step son. I started feeling compassion for him; I was feeling the empathy my ex-husband wished for while I lived with them. I was no longer livid at my Dad. God, through this 12 Step program, helped me see that my father was suffering just like I was. We shared the same sickness.

After the Holy Spirit called me into church and I started doing bible studies, my prayers changed again. I no longer ask Him to look out for me, because I know He does this without my asking. In Hebrews 13:5 it states keep your life free from love of money, and be content with what you have; for he has said, "I will never fail you nor forsake you." Each morning before I get out of bed, I thank Him for another new day. I thank Him for looking after me. I thank Him for giving us Jesus. I thank Jesus for dying on the cross for our sins. Each morning I pray that I am open to his guidance so I may better do His will. His will, not mine, be done. The Big

Book suggests we ask for the freedom from self-will, and are careful to make no request for ourselves only. We may ask for ourselves, however, if others will be helped. We are careful never to pray for our own selfish ends.

We are all on our own journeys with God. I decided to get baptized after a sermon explaining we have to get our sinful self out of the way so God can work in us. That was what this 12 Step process did for me. It helps us identify the truth from the false. It helps us take ownership of ourselves. It helps us let go and let God take over.

Through prayer we talk to God. Through meditation we listen to God.

I started reading the Bible. Front to back. It took forty years for God to lead His people out of Egypt because they kept doing the same thing over and over expecting different results. He would perform miracle after miracle, yet they still wanted to go back to Egypt. Aren't we the same? Don't we go back to the same old environment or routine because we're comfortable there?

Walking or hiking in natural surroundings allows me to listen and talk to God. Our earth has so many majestic creations; from the peaks of Mt. Everest down to a cocoon turning into a beautiful butterfly. Creating is a form of meditation for me. I'm making quilts to raise money for domestic violence. Sometimes I'll listen to a sermon or a recovery message while sewing, other times I enjoy the quiet.

Before I acknowledged God, He connected me with Melody Beattie, author of *Codependent No More*. I've read many of her books, but the title *Make Miracles in Forty Days* changed my journaling to grateful journals. I've kept a personal one, but I've also done Project Miracle with a friend. One of my journals had a highlight of the day placeholder box for a picture or a keepsake. I filled those boxes with scripture from the Bible.

In Ephesians 3:16-19 it states that according to the riches of his glory he may grant you to be strengthened with might through his Spirit in the inner man, and that Christ may dwell in your hearts through faith; that you, being rooted and grounded in love, may have power to comprehend with all the saints what is the breadth and length and height and depth, and to know the love of Christ which surpasses knowledge, that you may be filled with all the fullness of God.

*S*he walks to the back of the room again, but this time she pours herself a coffee. With her coffee in hand, she finishes her circle down the center aisle, back to the podium. She pauses as she looks at the each of the faces staring back at her. She makes eye contact with each and every one of them. Some immediately look away feeling uncomfortable. She remembers when she didn't have the courage to look others straight in the eye. She'd look at their noses or watch their mouths move as they talked, but never into their eyes.

"And now Step 12 says, having had a spiritual awakening as a result of these steps, we tried to carry this message to alcoholics and to practice these principles in all our affairs. I use the word others in place of the word alcoholics because I believe everyone can benefit from seeing the truth about themselves and having the wonderful experience of a spiritual awakening. The Bible verse for Step 12 is Galatians 6:1, brethren, if a man is overtaken in any trespass, you who are spiritual should restore him in a spirit of gentleness. Look to yourself, lest you too be tempted. If we reach Step 12 we are as stated in Galatians 2:20. We are crucified with Christ (our Higher Power); it is no longer I who live, but Christ (my Higher Power)who lives in me; and the life I now live in the flesh I live by faith in the Son of God (my Higher Power), who loved me and gave himself for me. In Romans 8:28 it says we know that in everything God works for good with those who love him, who are called according to his purpose. In Step 12 He calls us according to his purpose. We took that oath in Step 3 with our Third Step prayer.

Another verse in the Bible, Hebrews 10:23-25, encourages us to let us hold fast the confession of our hope without wavering, for he who promised is faithful; and let us consider how to stir up one another to love and good works, not neglecting to meet together, as is the habit of some, but encouraging one another, and all the more as you see the Day drawing near.

Jesus said in John 8:31-32, "If you continue in my word, you are truly my disciples, and you will know the truth, and the truth will make you free." We are his disciples. Through our past experience, through our spiritual awakening, we are now His to do His work in healing others.

First of all, what is a spiritual awakening? I describe mine like this: I had a childhood dream, a passion, for a better life. Something inside me kept telling me that my childhood life was not what life was supposed to be. I wanted, as I told you at the beginning, a normal life. I wanted peace. I wanted serenity. I wanted happiness, health and prosperity. I entered the recovery program because I saw it as another self-help group willing to modify my behavior. I saw myself as broken and needing to be fixed. What a surprise I got! My childhood dream came true.

I give all the glory to God; He led me through my journey and I have experienced Grace.

How is the message of a spiritual awakening carried to others?

We share our stories. We share experience, strength and hope. We share the Word. In the walls of recovery and in church, we introduce ourselves to newcomers and offer our phone number. If we're lucky, the new person will call. New people in recovery are not familiar with asking for help, so we all pray for them. We are all thankful they walked through the door; it's their first step in looking for help.

We listen. We hear the stories of loneliness and despair which are all too familiar. We want to give the new comer hope that peace and serenity and love will come as they work the program. We tell them that we followed the guidance of a sponsor; we did what they said and a miracle happened. People expect the process to be complicated. It's not. The sponsor reads the Big Book of Alcoholics Anonymous to the new person and shares experience, strength and hope. My sponsor told me she was a conduit for God to work through her. We read His Word to others and teach the doctrines. We all become a channel for God. And then watch God at work.

What principles do we practice in all our affairs?

The first principles we practice are to admit we are powerless and to be willing to believe in a power greater than ourselves. As we grow, we use these steps as a way of life. You can literally think of the 12 Steps as a set of stairs; we go up and down them many times in the course of our lives. We may go up and down the stairs many times in the course of a day. I constantly find myself going back to Step 1 and surrendering.

Just recently, my little four legged companion got attacked by a larger dog. She had to go to emergency surgery to be cleaned up and to have the 10-11 puncture wounds stitched and drained. I thought I might lose her, but she didn't have any broken bones or internal damage. I wanted this guy to pay. He didn't even act sorry which raised the hair on the back of my neck a little. He answered my first two calls, made an appointment to meet me to settle up and never showed. He stopped answering my calls.

I went right back into my old behavior. I was fighting back. However, I am a child of God and I listened when He spoke to me. It was okay to hold this man accountable, but you need to practice these principles in all your affairs. Are you practicing these? I left him another message and told him that he had a responsibility regarding the event, but God loved him regardless of how he chose to deal with the incident.

The principles: Honesty, Hope, Faith, Courage, Integrity, Willingness, Humility, Brotherly Love, Justice, Perseverance, Spiritual Awareness, and Service.

Carrying His message is sometimes as simple as loving someone; showing up; making a commitment. Prior to giving God permission to enter into our hearts, our love for others was conditional. We believed we would receive more love by putting conditions on it; however, whatever we give to others we get back in return. It may not be in the form you expect, but brace yourself, because God lets us truly experience the word abundance.

In Matthew 22:36-39 Jesus was asked, "Teacher, which is the great commandment in the law?" And he said to him, "You shall love the Lord your God with all your heart, and with all your soul, and with all your mind. This is the great and first commandment. And a second is like it, You shall love your neighbor as yourself." The Bible also states in John 14:15, if you love me, you will keep my commandments. Then later in John 15:10 the Bible states, If you keep my commandments, you will abide in my love, just as I have kept my Father's commandments and abide in his love. and in John 15:12, this is my commandment that you love one another as I have loved you.

In closing today, I would like to share Romans 5:1-5. Therefore, since we are justified by faith, we have peace with

God through our Lord Jesus Christ. Through him we have obtained access to this grace in which we stand, and we rejoice in our hope of sharing the glory of God. More than that, we rejoice in our sufferings, knowing that suffering produces endurance, and endurance produces character, and character produces hope, and hope does not disappoint us, because God's love has been poured into our hearts through the Holy Spirit which has been given to us. And finally, The Big Book also says many could recover if they had the opportunity we have enjoyed. How then shall we present that which has been so freely given us?

Thank you so much for coming."

The facilitator steps to the podium and shakes Leanne's hand while he thanks her. He turns to the group and says, "For all of those who are willing, we would like to make a circle holding hands and repeat the Lord's Prayer." Chairs start scraping across the floor as people stand, stretching. The couple gets up and joins the circle, but they stay together so they are holding each other's hands. The timekeeper nestles in next to Leanne, taking her hand and as soon as the circle is closed, the facilitator says, "Whose Father?"

Our Father, which art in heaven, Hallowed be thy Name.
Thy Kingdom come; Thy will be done on earth,
As it is in heaven.
Give us this day our daily bread.
And forgive us our trespasses,
As we forgive those that trespass against us.
And lead us not into temptation,
But deliver us from evil.
For thine is the kingdom, The power, and the glory, Forever.
Amen.

References

Alcoholics Anonymous, Third Edition. Copyright 1939, 1955, 1976 by Alcoholics Anonymous World Services, Inc

The Holy Bible, Revised Standard Edition. Copyright 1962 by the World Publishing Company

Revised Standard Version of the Bible, copyright © 1946, 1952, and 1971 the Division of Christian Education of the National Council of the Churches of Christ in the United States of America.

Practice These Principles and What is the Oxford Group? Copyright 1997 by Hazelden Foundation

Serenity :a companion for twelve step recovery Copyright 1990 by Thomas Nelson, Inc.

Make Miracles in Forty Days, Melody Beattie. Copyright 2010 by Melody and Company, Inc.

http://www.acadv.org/children.html Alabama Coalition Against Domestic Violence

http://www.aafp.org American Academy of American Physician

Index